# PAUL S. SCHUDER
## Science Collections

## Woodland Public Library

Mimbres design from Art of a Vanished Race

# SAVING THE CONDOR

# SAVING THE CONDOR

## BY NANCY T. SCHORSCH

FRANKLIN WATTS
NEW YORK LONDON TORONTO SYDNEY
A FIRST BOOK 1991

Cover photograph courtesy of: National Audubon Society (Jesse Grantham)

Photographs courtesy of: National Audubon Society/U.S. Fish and Wildlife Service: pp. 2 (Victor Apanius), 8 (Leon Hecht), 10 (John McNeely), 18 (David Clendenen), 20 bottom, 43, 58 (Victor Apanius); National Audubon Society: pp. 12 (Helen Snyder), 15 top, 16 (Virgil Ketner), 22 (John C. Ogden), 30, 34 (Helen Snyder), 39 (David Clendenen); Zoological Society of San Diego: pp. 13, 20 top, 41, 45, 48, 49, 50, 56 (all Ron Garrison), 24 (Craig W. Racicot), 46 (F. D. Schmidt), 53; American Museum of Natural History: p. 27; U.S. Fish and Wildlife Service: 36 (Fred C. Sibley); David W. Johnson: p. 55.

Library of Congress Cataloging-in-Publication Data

Schorsch, Nancy T.
Saving the condor / by Nancy T. Schorsch.
p.     cm. — (A First book)
Includes bibliographical references and index.
Summary: Tells the story of biologists' efforts to save the last
California condors from extinction by breeding them in captivity and
returning them to the wild.
ISBN 0-531-20010-8
1. California condor—Juvenile literature.   2. Birds. Protection
of—California—Juvenile literature. [1. California condor.
2. Condors.   3. Rare birds.   4. Birds—Protection.   5. Wildlife
conservation.]   I. Title.   II. Series.
OL696.F33S36   1991
639.9′78912—dc20          90-47518   CIP   AC

# CONTENTS

**1**

AC-9, the Last Wild Condor

9

**2**

The Condor in the Wild

17

**3**

The Early History of
Humans and the Condor

26

**4**

Humans' Effect on the Condor

32

**5**

Humans Try to Save the Condor

38

**6**

The Future of the Condor

52

For Further Reading

60

Index

62

An adult California
condor soars across
the skies in a
protected sanctuary.

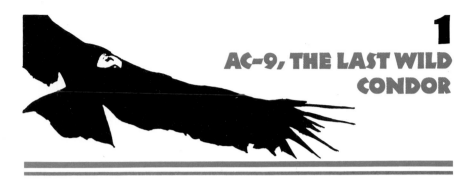

# 1
# AC-9, THE LAST WILD CONDOR

AC-9 soared across the wild, rugged mountains, looking for his mate, looking for other birds of his kind. He could not find any, and flew alone across the California skies.

AC-9 was alone because all the other birds like him had been trapped and taken into captivity. For a month, wildlife biologists had been tracking AC-9, putting food in several different spots to attract him. He was a curious and very clever bird, hopping around the bait set out for him, but never coming close enough to be caught. The game of hide-and-seek went on.

Then, on Easter Sunday, April 19, 1987, AC-9 appeared at a feeding spot. His behavior had changed—he acted differently this time, almost as though he wanted to be caught. He flew down to the goat carcass

In 1987, biologists successfully captured
AC-9 by using a cannon net.

that had been put out for him as bait, and started to feed. Suddenly, from a pit nearby, a hidden cannon exploded and shot out a net. It covered him and held him to the ground.

AC-9, the last wild California condor, had been caught. For the first time in 15,000 years, the largest bird in North America no longer flew over the mountains and valleys of central and southern California.

The biologists who caught AC-9 moved quickly to calm him. They carefully placed the giant bird in a portable shelter and took him to the San Diego Wild Animal Park. Here he was kept in quarantine for two weeks so veterinarians could make sure he was healthy. They found that he was in good shape, so they moved him to a large enclosure called a "condorminium," a place he could share with other members of his species. He was later moved to the Los Angeles Zoo, where he now lives with other condors.

AC-9 will never be allowed to fly free again, but will be kept in captivity and used in an exciting new breeding program. His chicks will be raised at the zoo, and if all goes as planned, they will be released into the wild in the near future.

AC-9 was well known to biologists. On May 14, 1980, they watched through a telescope as a half mile away the baby bird pecked at his shell and broke it open.

An aerial view of the "condorminium"
in the San Diego Wild Animal Park
Left: an Audubon biologist with a
California condor during a 1982
successful trapping

It was the first time anyone had seen a condor chick hatch. They watched as his parents took turns feeding him. He was a healthy chick and grew bigger and stronger each day. They watched as he sat on the branch of a tree near his nest and tried flapping his wings, finally flying for the first time that November.

In 1984, biologists managed to put a small radio transmitter on one of AC-9's wings, then let him go. This tracking device made it possible to know where he was at all times, to learn how far he flew and where he went to feed. He was the most closely watched of all condors.

Biologists called him IC-9 at first, for immature condor, and gave him the number 9 because he was the ninth condor to be radio-tagged.

When he was five years old, he mated with an older female, AC-8, whose mate had died the year before. She chose him over two older males. His name was then changed to AC-9, or Adult Condor-9.

In the spring of 1986, AC-8 laid an egg which was found broken in the nest. The next month she laid

A California condor
hatchling in the wild

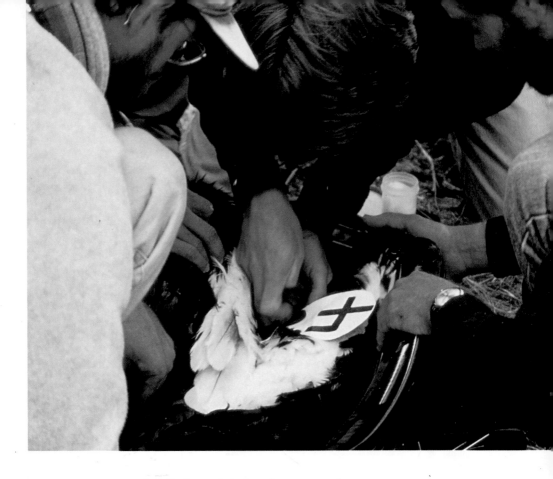

Audubon biologists attach
a radio transmitter and tag to
California condor IC-4 in 1984.

another. This second egg was taken from the nest and
was hatched successfully at the San Diego Wild Animal
Park. AC-8 was captured on the same day in June of
1986 that her chick hatched, and she is now in the
condorminium at the San Diego Wild Animal Park.

# THE CONDOR IN THE WILD

AC-9 and all other California condors belong to the vulture family. These gigantic birds weigh as much as 25 pounds (about 11 kg), are 4 feet long (about 1.22 m) from head to tail, and are more than 9 feet (about 2.74 m) from wingtip to wingtip. A bald eagle or a turkey vulture looks small when compared to a condor.

Adult condors have gray-black feathers, and when they fly you can see a large white patch under each wing. The head and neck are orange and have no feathers. They are magnificent fliers and can soar on air currents without flapping their wings for hours at a time. They circle up on warm air currents as high as 15,000 feet (4,572 m) and can reach flying speeds as great as 35

An adult California condor with its characteristic orange head and neck and brilliant red eyes

miles per hour (about 56 kph). They also fly great distances looking for food, sometimes traveling nearly 100 miles (about 161 k) in a day in their search.

Condors are not able to kill their prey, so they feed on carrion, the bodies of dead animals. They like to eat deer, cattle, sheep, or goats, but they will eat smaller animals such as squirrels or coyotes. There are even reports from long ago of condors eating salmon along the rivers in the American Northwest.

Sometimes, when condors find a large kill, they eat so much that they are too heavy to fly. They jump to a low branch where they sit, often for hours, until their food digests. Only then can they take off and fly.

After eating, the birds clean their bare heads and necks by rubbing them in grass. They also find clear pools of water in the mountains where they bathe.

Adult condors in the wild mate for life when they are about five to eight years old. Only if one condor dies does the other take a new mate, as when AC-8 chose AC-9. In early spring, the female looks for a place to lay her single egg. Condors do not build a nest, but find a high, safe place for their eggs, usually a cave in a cliff. Some birds nest in large holes high up in the trunk of a giant sequoia tree. They choose safe places, away from their enemies. Ravens will eat condor eggs, and golden eagles will take condor chicks out of their nests. Biolo-

gists once even watched as a bear tried to steal an egg from a condor nest, but the condor had made its nest too high for the bear to reach. AC-9 hatched from an egg laid by his mother on the sandy floor of a small cave high on a cliff.

In the wild, condors usually lay only one egg every other year. The eggs are pale blue-green, weigh about 8 (226 grams) ounces, and are over 4 inches (10 cm) long and about 2 inches (5 cm) in diameter. Both parents take turns sitting on the egg, and in fifty-six to sixty days the egg hatches.

When the young chick hatches from the egg, its skin is pink and is covered with soft, white down feathers, except for its head and neck, which are bare. It then gets a second coat of gray, woolly down over all but its head and neck.

Condor parents take good care of their one chick. One parent stays in the nest with the baby condor while its mate flies out in search of food. Food is sometimes hard to find and the parent must fly long distances in

Top: two California condors engaging in courtship behavior

Bottom: a typical California condor nesting habitat high in a cliff

search of a dead animal to feed on. The parent might be gone from the nest for more than a day, but the nest is never left unguarded except for a few minutes when the adult in the nest flies out to meet its mate coming in with food. The parent flies to the nest and regurgitates the food into the mouth of the chick or onto the floor of the cave.

Regular feathers start to develop on the young condor when it is about seven weeks old. It takes more than five months before it has all the feathers it needs to fly. A condor chick makes its first flight when it is about six or seven months old. The chick will stay with its parents for up to a year after leaving the nest, which explains why adults nest and have young only every other year.

Condors once were found all the way from western Canada to Baja California. Now their range is only in central and southern California. Fossils of condors have been found as far east as Florida and New York, but they may not be the same species as the modern condor.

There probably never were great numbers of condors, but since scientists have been keeping records, their numbers have steadily decreased.

California condor AC-9's
parents at his nest site in 1980

All living California condors are now in captivity, one flock at the Los Angeles Zoo and the other at the San Diego Wild Animal Park. Their numbers are at last increasing, and the outlook for the condor is better now than it has been for many years.

California condor chick Molloko
at about six months of age

# 3
# THE EARLY HISTORY OF HUMANS AND THE CONDOR

AC-9 and the other condors before him have a long history of contact with human beings. The efforts to save the condor today are the result of a fascination people have had with the condor for a long time.

Condors and human beings have shared the same territory for thousands of years. It is believed that humans came to North America from Asia, across to what is now Alaska. When they traveled south through Canada to the northwestern part of the United States they saw condors flying.

They might even have seen the two possible ancestors of the modern California condor. The earliest of these birds, *Teratornis incredibilis*, had a wingspan of 17 feet (about 5 m) and was probably the largest bird ever to fly. A later form, *Gymnogyps amplus*, was closer to

A historical painting shows an
early ancestor of the
modern California condor.

the modern condor. He shared the earth with saber-toothed tigers, dire wolves, mastodons, and mammoths. Their bones are found together in the famous La Brea Tar Pits of Los Angeles. The large mammals, thinking the tar pits were pools of water, went to them to drink. They were trapped by the sticky tar and could not escape. The birds flew down to feed on the large animals, got stuck in the tar, and couldn't fly away. They sank into the tar pits and died with the other animals.

The first written report of condors appeared about four hundred years ago in the diary of Father Ascension, a Spanish missionary. He was on one of three ships exploring the western coast of America. As his ship sailed along the coast of central California, he spotted a group of the giant vultures feeding on the carcass of a whale washed up on the shore. Father Ascension was so impressed by the big birds that he wrote this about them in his journal:

> *There are some other birds of the shape of turkeys, the largest I saw on this voyage. From the point of one wing to that of the other it was found to measure seventeen spans.*

Seventeen spans is the equivalent of 11 feet 4 inches (about 3.4 m). Such large birds must certainly have been condors.

The earliest account we have of Indians and condors comes from an overland Spanish expedition on its way through California. The explorers wrote about a large "eagle" in an Indian village just south of what is now San Francisco. The bird measured 7 feet 4 inches (about 2.5 m) from wingtip to wingtip. The report stated:

> *We saw in this place a bird which the heathen had killed and stuffed with straw: to some of our party it looked like a royal eagle. It was measured from tip to tip of the wings and found to measure eleven spans.*

The Spaniards had been camping by a river, and were so impressed by the large bird that they named the river "Pajaro," which means bird in Spanish.

The most important festival of the year for the Indians of southern California was the "panes," or bird feast. The Indians of this area believed in the legend of a young girl who had run off to the mountains and been turned into a bird. They thought that this was the same bird they sacrificed every year, coming back to life after it had been killed.

Condors were also used for funerals. In ceremonies honoring the dead, the Indians wore headbands of condor feathers and carried sacred poles decorated with

The Chumash Indians believed that
"magic condor feathers" held the
power to find lost objects
and missing people.

condor feathers. Condors were sometimes sacrificed as a part of burial ceremonies among some tribes. Archeologists have found condor bones buried with human remains in many parts of the West. In fact, the majority of condor bones that have been excavated were located in connection with human home or burial sites.

# 4
# HUMANS' EFFECT
# ON THE
# CONDOR

Before Europeans came to western America, the area was populated by small groups of Indians scattered over a large area. Although the native tribes did kill some condors to use in their ceremonies, they respected the condor as a sacred bird. As a result, the population of the condor was not greatly affected. This changed when the Spaniards settled in California.

Soon after the first settlers established towns and missions, reports were sent back to Spain. People were fascinated by this new land, and were curious about the new forms of life being found there. Reports of the new animals were of special interest to the Europeans. Before long, collectors came to the West to find and take home samples.

The first California condor put into a scientific collection was killed and skinned by a British scientist in 1792. At that time it was given its scientific name, *Gymnogyps californianus*.

One thing the Europeans brought with them that the Indians did not have was the gun. When these new people came west to explore and settle, they started shooting condors. The birds were such large targets that it was easy to kill them. And people thought it was great sport to fire at the large birds. Young condors like AC-9 were known for being curious, and would often fly in close to investigate people coming into their territory.

Humans and guns have caused the deaths of many condors in the past, and although in modern times there have been several other causes, they are all related to humans.

It is difficult to trace the reasons for the deaths of many condors. They live in rugged, remote areas hard to reach by man. They fly great distances and are hard to follow. In recent years, when a condor carcass has been found, it has been sent to a museum or laboratory so that scientists could try to determine why the bird died. Some had eaten deer that had been shot, and had died of lead poisoning from swallowing the lead bullet fragments. The poison dissolved and went through the body of the condor, poisoning the tissue.

Some dead condors were found in areas where poi-

son had been put out to kill squirrels or coyotes. They probably died from eating the poisoned animals. Another cause of death has been collisions with power lines built in the areas where condors fly.

About a hundred years ago, egg collecting was a popular hobby that caused the loss of many condors. Collectors all over the world would pay high prices for the eggs of rare birds, and the California condor egg was a prize for such collectors. One collector was paid three hundred dollars for a single condor egg.

In more recent times, condor eggs might have suffered from a man-made chemical. When AC-9's mate laid its first egg in the cliff cave, biologists climbed up to check on it. They found a very thin broken shell. In a laboratory they discovered that the egg shell contained a form of DDT which had probably gotten into the mother condor's body from its food supply. DDT has caused many other wild birds to lay eggs with thin shells. The mother's weight was probably enough to break the egg when she tried to sit on it. It is possible

Frost has settled on the corpse
of California condor IC-1.
IC-1 died from lead poisoning.

that in recent years other adult condors have lost eggs in the same way.

Humans and their activities seem to be the main enemy of the condor, from ancient Indian sacrifice to modern guns and poisons. If humans had left the California condor alone in its range over western valleys and mountains, it probably would still be flying free today.

A California condor sits protectively on a nest.

# 5
# HUMANS TRY TO SAVE THE CONDOR

As the years passed, the condor population continued to decline. If condors were to be saved, humans had to do it. Humans had been the cause of the condors' disappearance from the skies, and now had to make an effort to save this unique and wonderful creature.

Experts believed that by protecting condor nest areas, the birds could be saved. If condors could raise their young in a place far from human activity, their numbers might increase.

One of the first efforts to protect the condor was made in 1946. A sanctuary, or safe place, was set aside in one of the condor nesting areas. There was to be no hunting allowed, and roads and mining activity were to be kept as far from the condors as possible. Even pilots were told not to fly too close to the condor territory.

38

The eastern part of the
Sespe Condor Sanctuary \

Over the years, the sanctuary has been enlarged and other protected areas have been set aside for the birds.

Scientists thought they had created a safe place for the condors to live and nest, but this wasn't so. Condors nest in very rugged areas to protect their eggs and young from their enemies. Their food supply is far from their nests, so they must travel long distances to find food, often flying over areas where there is a danger of being shot. There is also a danger of eating contaminated food—carcasses that are poisoned or contain lead bullets.

Biologists tried putting out safe carcasses near the nesting sites, hoping the condors would eat them. But the condors continued to feed the way they had been feeding for thousands of years. Older birds had taught the young where to find food, and they continued flying into dangerous areas in search of food.

During the 1960s and 1970s, more attempts were made to save the condor. The government passed laws declaring the condor an endangered species in need of protection. But it was difficult to patrol such a huge area, and hunters and ranchers could still legally shoot deer and poison unwanted animals. The number of condors continued to fall.

There were different opinions and many arguments about the best way to deal with the condor problem. Many experts felt that the birds should be left to fly free

California condor Sisquoc
feeding on an animal carcass

in the wild at all costs, even if all the condors died. They felt that a condor in a cage was worse than a dead condor. Others felt that people should save the remaining birds by taking some into captivity, raising them, and eventually releasing some into the wild.

By 1980, there were fewer than thirty birds in the wild, and the flock was decreasing. In 1982, three things happened that changed the circumstances of the California condor.

A chick was discovered in a nest with only one parent. The other parent had disappeared. Biologists feared that the chick was not getting enough to eat and would not survive. Permission was granted to capture the baby bird. It was successfully brought into captivity and survived.

Two years earlier, biologists had tried to handle another chick while it was in the nest. The baby bird died while it was being weighed and measured. The death of that chick so alarmed many people that permits to handle young condors were denied. The survival of the second chick proved that with proper handling the chicks could be brought into captivity.

Also in 1982 it was shown definitely that if an egg is removed from a condor nest, the birds will mate again and the female will lay a second egg. Sometimes even a third egg will be laid if the second is taken. The eggs that

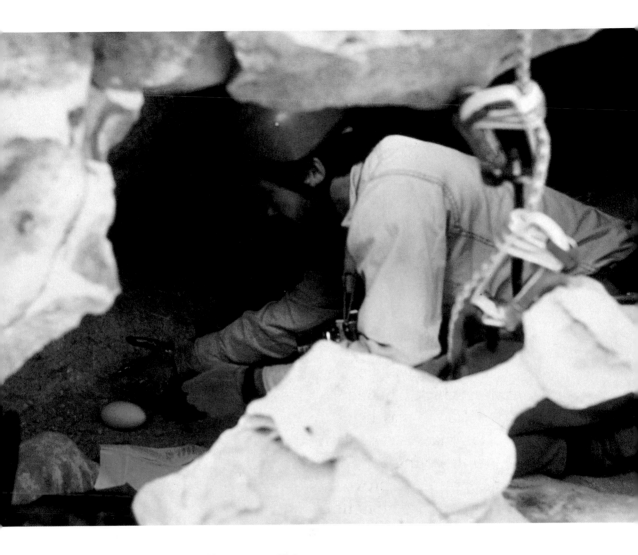

A biologist collects a wild
condor egg for the captive
breeding flock.

were taken were hatched in captivity and the birds are living today.

Finally, late in 1982, the first two condors were captured and fitted with radio transmitters. Wildlife biologists could now track the birds and learn more about their habits.

For the next two years, many eggs were taken from nests and successfully hatched in captivity. Some young wild chicks were also brought in and successfully raised in captivity. If a chick was taken, the adult would lay an egg every year instead of every other year. It was hoped that there would be many more wild birds, and the captive flock was growing and thriving. There was even talk of releasing some of the captive birds to increase the wild flock.

But during the winter of 1984 to 1985, disaster struck. When biologists started looking for nesting pairs of condors in early 1985, they discovered only single birds in the nesting areas. The mates were nowhere to be found. After several months of searching for the birds, it was found that six of the remaining

California condor chick Molloko
successfully hatching in captivity.

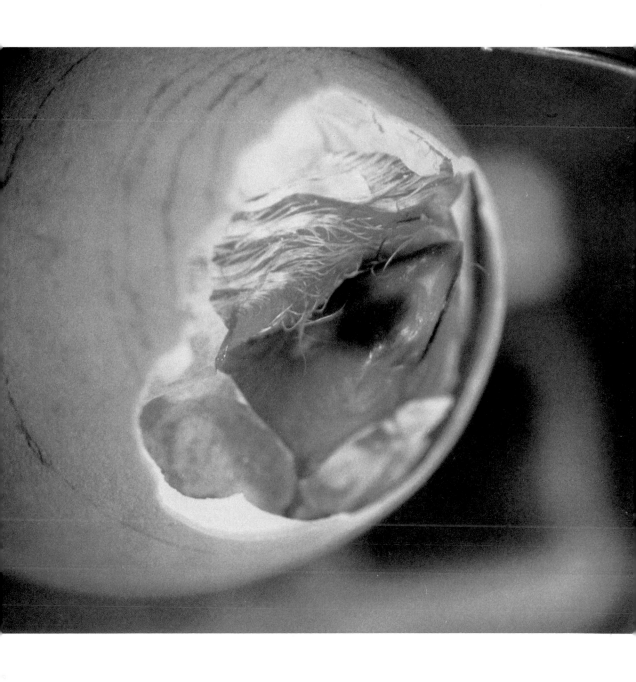

California condor chick Sisquoc
when only twelve hours old

fifteen wild condors had died over the winter. So few birds were now left in the wild that the following winter the decision was made to capture them before they, too, were lost.

From the fall of 1986 to the spring of 1987, biologists in the field tried to locate and capture all the wild condors. AC-9 was the last bird to be brought in on that April day in 1987.

The survival of the condor was now in the hands of biologists at the San Diego Wild Animal Park and the Los Angeles Zoo. The captive flock was growing. Biologists had had great success hatching eggs taken from nests in the wild. Between 1983 and 1986, thirteen eggs had hatched.

After the capture of all the wild condors, there were no more eggs to be brought in. What scientists did not know was whether the birds would mate and lay eggs in captivity. Although other vultures had mated in captivity and many young had hatched from their eggs, no one knew about the California condor. Pairs of birds were put together, and during the winter of 1987 to 1988 one pair started showing some courtship behavior. In the spring of 1988 the female laid an egg, which was taken from the mother and put in an incubator. About two months later a healthy chick was hatched. The following year four chicks were hatched from the

seven eggs laid by several females. In 1990 more chicks were hatched.

The keepers feed the chicks with hand puppets that look just like adult condors, to keep the birds from getting used to receiving food from humans. The chicks are fed minced mice and food regurgitated by other vultures. As they grow older, they are put into large enclosures with other condors. This way they interact with other members of their species rather than adapting to human beings.

AC-9 is paired at the Los Angeles Zoo with a female that was taken into captivity in 1984. AC-8 is paired at the San Diego Wild Animal Park with AC-5, the bird captured a month before AC-9 was taken in. These two birds produced a healthy chick in 1989. And in 1990, AC-8 laid three eggs, all of which produced chicks.

Two-week-old
California condor
chick Molloko
with the puppet
used as a parent
and a feeder

The captive breeding program is a huge success so far. As the young birds become adults and more pairs are formed, it is hoped that each spring will bring many more condor chicks.

California condor chick
Sisquoc learning to fly

Plans for the future release of California condors into the wild are being made with special care. Scientists do not want to send condors back to the wild to face the same hazards that caused them to die in the past. They want to be certain that the birds will successfully live and raise their young.

Biologists believed that they could release condors into a known nesting area, with plenty of uncontaminated food. With this food supply, the birds would not search out food in other more dangerous places. And there would be no adult birds in the wild to teach the young condors bad habits.

Scientists wanted to try a release program, but didn't want to risk losing condors. They decided to try the plan on the South American Andean condor, a close

An adult South
American Andean
condor

relative of the California condor. The Andean condor is very similar in looks and habits to its California cousin. The males are a little larger than the California condor, but the females are about the same size. In the wild they fly over the Andes Mountains of western South America. Even though they are endangered in their native territory, there are many more Andean than California condors because they have been raised in captivity for years. Some captive birds have even been released back into the wild in South America, where they have adapted very well, joining the wild birds and surviving.

Since there were many Andean birds available for the experiment, in 1988 a two-year plan got under way. One group of six Andean condors was released in the fall of that year. A second group was taken out the following year and put into the wild. Only females were used because scientists did not want the Andean condors to breed and start a new colony in California.

The birds were taken to a remote area of a condor sanctuary, carried in covered cages at night so they would not see the humans handling them. They were all very young birds covered with fluffy down feathers, and had not yet learned to fly. They were put in a "roost box," a pen with a feeding platform next to it. Food was put out for them in the dark so they could not see the humans feeding them. The entire box was covered with a net so the birds could not escape.

A South American Andean condor
paces in its "roost box."

The Andean condors stayed in their enclosure for several months to get used to the area. When they flapped their wings and showed that they were ready to fly, the scientists removed the net. The condors were free, and immediately began to explore their new territory. They flew first to stumps nearby and then took longer and longer flights away from their roost box.

The birds did exactly what biologists had expected them to do. All of the Andean condors were fitted with radio transmitters so that they could be tracked. As time passed, they traveled greater and greater distances, up to seventy miles (about 113 km) from where they had been released. The birds did not look for food outside the sanctuary, but always came back to their feeding area and ate only the food put out for them.

The Andean condors will be left in the wild for two years, after which they will be recaptured. They will then be taken to the Andes Mountains of South America and released into their native habitat.

Scientists plan to release California condors into the same wild area where the Andean birds were. The An-

A South American Andean condor
outfitted with a radio transmitter
for tracking its movements

An adult California condor
sunning at a protected roost site

dean condor experiment has shown that the birds can be released safely.

Only young condors hatched in captivity will be released. The older birds taken from the wild, including AC-9, will be kept in Los Angeles or San Diego to produce chicks for years to come. A few condors held in zoos have lived to be very old, and experts are hopeful that these condors will live for many more years.

Once the birds are in the wild, humans will continue to put out clean food in safe feeding spots. The condors will get used to feeding only in these places, and will not wander away to look for food in dangerous areas.

They will be in territory where other condors have lived in the past. There are good nesting places for them, and they will be able to lay their eggs and raise their young in the safety of this sanctuary.

The largest bird in North America, the magnificent California condor, will again be soaring on the air currents over the wild and rugged terrain of California. Future generations of human beings will be able to enjoy the beauty of their flight for many years.

# FOR FURTHER READING

Catchpole, Clive. *Birds of Prey That Hunt by Day*. New York: McGraw-Hill, 1977.

Coombs, Charles. *Soaring: Where Hawks and Eagles Fly*. New York: Henry Holt & Company, 1988.

Dewitt, Linda. *Eagles, Hawks, and Other Birds of Prey*. New York: Franklin Watts, 1989.

Hoffman, Mary. *Birds of Prey*. Milwaukee: Raintree Publications, 1987.

Hogner, Dorothy Childs. *Birds of Prey*. New York: Crowell, 1969.

Jennings, Terry. *Birds*. Chicago: Children's Division of Regensteiner Publishing Enterprise, 1984.

Lentz, Joan E., and Judith Young. *Birdwatching, A Guide for Beginners*. Santa Barbara, Calif.: Capra Press, 1985.

National Geographic Society. *Field Guide to the Birds of North America*. Washington, D.C.: National Geographic Society, 1987.

Peterson, Roger Tory. *Peterson's First Guide to Birds*. Boston: Houghton Mifflin, 1986.

Petty, Kate. *Birds of Prey*. New York: Franklin Watts, 1987.

Turner, Ann Warren. *Vultures*. New York: David McKay, 1973.

Page numbers in *italics* refer to illustrations.

Ascension, Father, 28

California condor
    attempts to save, 48–51
    in captivity, 25, 42–51, *45*, 59
    coloring of, 17, *18*
    courtship and mating of, 19, *20*, 47
    deaths of, 33–37, *34*, 44–47
    early history of humans and, 26–31
    eggs of, 21, 35–37, 42–44, *43*, 47–49
    as endangered species, 40
    feathers of, 17, 21, 23, 29–31, *30*
    feeding of, 19, 21–23, 40, *41*, *48*, 49, 52, 57, 59
    first written report of, 28

flying of, 17–19, 23, 50

fossils of, 23

future of, 25, 52–59

grooming of, 19

humans' effect on, 32–37

last in wild, 9–14, 10, 47

nesting of, 19–21, 20, 22, 36, 38–40

numbers of, 23–25, 42, 44–47

parenting of, 21–23

possible ancestors of, 26–28, 27

range of, 23

releasing into wild, 52–59

sanctuaries for, 8, 38–40, 39

scientific name of, 33

size of, 17, 28

trapping of, 9–11, 10, 12

California condor
   chicks, 15, 21–23, 24, 46
   hatching of, 11–14, 21, 42–44, 45, 47–49
   raising in captivity, 42, 44, 48, 49, 50

Chumash Indians, 30

Condors
   South American
      Andean, 52–57, 53, 55, 56
   See also California
      condor

Courtship behavior, 19, 20, 47

DDT, 35–37

Eggs, 11–14, 21, 35–37
   hatched in captivity, 16, 42–44, 45, 47–49
   laying of, 42, 44, 47

Feathers, 17, 21, 23, 29–31, *30*
Feeding behavior, 19, 21–23, 40, *41*
in captivity, *48,* 49
release programs and, 52, 57, 59
Flying, 17–19, 23, *50*
Fossils, 23

Grooming behavior, 19
Guns, 33, 37
*Gymnogyps amplus,* 26–28
*Gymnogyps californianus,* 33

Hatching, 11–14, 21
in captivity, 16, 42–44, *45,* 47–49

Indians, 29–31, *30,* 32, 33, 37

La Brea Tar Pits, 28
Los Angeles Zoo, 11, 25, 47, 49, 59

Mating behavior, 19, *20,* 47

Nests, 19–21, *20, 22, 36,* 38–40

Parenting behavior, 21–23
Poisons, 33–35, *34,* 37, 40

Radio transmitters, 14, *16,* 44, *56,* 57
Release programs, 52–59
"Roost boxes," 54–57, *55*

Sanctuaries, *8,* 38–40, *39*
San Diego Wild Animal Park, 11, *13,* 16, 25, 47, 49, 59
Sespe Condor Sanctuary, *39*
South American Andean condor, 52–57, *53, 55, 56*

*Teratornis incredibilis,* 26